PETS PLUS

Birds

Sally Morgan

D1497784

W
FRANKLIN WATTS
LONDON•SYDNEY

This edition published in 2013 by Franklin Watts

Franklin Watts
338 Euston Road, London NW1 3BH

Franklin Watts Australia
Level 17/207 Kent St, Sydney, NSW 2000

Created by Taglines Creative Ltd: www.taglinescreative.com
Author: Sally Morgan
Series designer: Hayley Cove
Editor: Jean Coppendale

ISBN: 978 1 4451 1848 2
Dewey classification: 636.6
A CIP catalogue record for this book is available from the British Library.

Picture credits
t=top b=bottom l=left r=right m=middle
Front cover: logo, Gouldian finch, Shutterstock/Eric Isselée; feathers, Shutterstock/mjf99; top, wild budgerigars, Shutterstock/KKulikov; bottom, pet budgerigars, Shutterstock/Yuri Shirokov;
Back cover: top, lorikeet, Shutterstock/Eric Isselée; bottom, house sparrow, Shutterstock/Vishnevskly Vasily
Title page: top, Shutterstock/Eric Isselée; Shutterstock/mjf99; left, parakeet, Ecoscene/Wayne Lawler; right, grey parrot, Ardea/John Daniels; Imprint page and top of spreads: house sparrow, Shutterstock/Vishnevskly Vasily; lorikeet, Shutterstock/Eric Isselée; p4l Ecoscene/Satyendra Tiwari, p4r Shutterstock/ simon/naffarts; p5t Ardea/John Paul Ferrero, p5b Shutterstock/Rob Byron; p6t Shutterstock/Nicky Rhodes, p6b Shutterstock/Guido Akster; p7l Ecoscene/Angela Hampton, p7t Shutterstock/Katrina Brown; p8 Ecoscene/Angela Hampton; p9t Shutterstock/Theodore Scott, p9b Shutterstock/Jill Young; p10l Shutterstock/Rob Byron, p10r Shutterstock/Thomas Skjaeveland; p11l Shutterstock/ Ecoprint; p11r iStock/Nicola Stratford; p12 Ecoscene/Angela Hampton; p13t Ecoscene/ Angela Hampton, p13b Ecoscene/Angela Hampton; p14 iStock/Sarah Bossert; p15t Shutterstock/Jasenka Luka, p15b Ecoscene/Angela Hampton; p16 iStock/ Webphotographer; p17l iStock/Glenn Jenkinson, p17r Shutterstock/Elena Elisseeva; p18 Ardea/Don Hadden; p19tl Shutterstock/Marina Jay, p19tm Shutterstock/Marina Jay, p19tr Shutterstock/Katrina Brown, p19b Shutterstock/ Vishnevskly Vasily; p20l Shutterstock/Jill Lang, p20r Ecoscene/Fritz Polking; p21 Shutterstock/ Sarycheva Olesia; p22 Shutterstock/J van der Wolf; p23tl Ecoscene/Wayne Lawler, p23tr Ecoscene/Angela Hampton, p23b Ecoscene/Angela Hampton; p24l Ecoscene/ Sally Morgan, p24r Shutterstock/Borislav Borisov; p25 Shutterstock/Bernd Schmidt; p26l Shutterstock/Boris 15, p26r Shutterstock/Gorschkov; p27l Shutterstock/ Pichugin Dimitry, p27tr Shutterstock/Nice Pictures, p27br Shutterstock/Christian Wilkinson; p28 Shutterstock/Elena Elisseeva; p29 Shutterstock/Jasenka Luka; p30 Shutterstock/Yuri Shirokov; p31 Shutterstock/K Kulikov

Printed in China

Franklin Watts is a division of Hachette
Children's Books, an Hachette UK company.
www.hachette.co.uk

Contents

The meaning of the words in **bold** can be found in the glossary.

pet birds, wild birds

Pet birds, such as chickens and budgerigars, are closely related to their wild cousins. Birds are kept as pets for fun.

Wild pets

People have kept birds for meat and eggs for thousands of years. Chickens living on farms and in gardens today have been **bred** from jungle fowl that lived in **tropical** forests of Asia. Pet ducks and geese have wild cousins, too.

Pet birds

Birds are kept as pets for many reasons. Some birds are kept for their sweet song, others because of their bright feathers and as company. However, birds are not as **domesticated** as dogs and cats, and they need to be **tamed**.

▼ This brightly coloured male jungle fowl (below) is related to the tame chickens (right) that many people keep for eggs.

Look alike

The feathers of many pet birds are the same colour as those of wild birds, for example pet grey parrots look just like wild grey parrots.

However, some pet birds, such as budgerigars, have been bred so that they have a bigger range of colours than wild birds.

▶ Wild budgerigars (right) are mostly green, while pet budgerigars (below) can be a variety of colours, including blue, yellow and even white.

Birds as pets

Birds make great pets. They can be friendly and chatty. Some love to play and learn tricks, while others love to have a cuddle.

Cage or aviary?

You can keep your pet in a cage in the house, but most cages are too small to allow a bird to fly. If you keep a bird in a cage, let it out to fly once a day. Some people keep pet birds outside in an **aviary**, which is a bird house big enough for them to fly about. An aviary needs shelter from wind, rain and sun, and a warm nest box for when it is cold.

▲ Many **macaws** have a **wingspan** of 100 cm or more, so the best place to keep a pet macaw (top) is in an outdoor aviary with plenty of space to fly, but these birds are not suitable for beginners.

Daily care

Many small birds are easy to look after, but some of the more **exotic** birds need special diets, and can catch diseases, which may also result in high vet's fees. Some birds, such as **cockatoos**, need lots of attention from their owner.

▶ Cockatoos are large, noisy birds that love company, but they are not suitable pets for beginners.

Buying your pet

If you buy your bird from a pet shop, make sure the birds look healthy and that their cages are clean. You can also buy birds from **breeders**. It is important to ask whether the animal was bred in **captivity**. Many exotic birds are caught in the wild and sold as pets. This trade is threatening the survival of wild birds.

▲ Choose a bird that is suitable for a beginner, such as a budgerigar or finch. A breeder will be able to advise you about which type of bird to buy and how to look after it.

PET POINT

Many wild birds live in flocks in the wild, and should not be kept alone. For example, canaries are best kept in pairs or small groups.

Which bird?

There is a huge choice of pet birds, from small finches to large macaws. Some species are easy to look after, but others need experience.

Large or small?

Some people choose a large, colourful bird such as a parrot or macaw. These make great pets but they are expensive to buy, and may be very noisy. They need a big cage and make a lot of mess. It is better to start off with small birds, such as canaries or lovebirds, that are cheaper and easier to look after.

Long lives

When you are choosing your pet, remember that many birds have long lives. A macaw may live for 100 years or more. The African grey parrot lives for 50 to 70 years, and a budgerigar about 25 years.

◀ This African grey parrot has a large cage with lots of toys. It also has a **perch** outside of the cage so it can fly around the room.

Easy care

Some birds, such as the colourful rainbow lorikeets, need a special diet of pollen and fruit. They produce runny droppings so their cages need a lot of cleaning. A better choice is a budgerigar or a finch. These birds are very colourful, need less space than many other birds and eat mostly seeds.

▲ **Zebra finches** are easy to look after but should be kept in pairs.

Playful parakeets

Parakeets are small parrots with long tail feathers. Some parakeets and parrots are very active. They love to play with toys. These birds also like to play with people, and enjoy company, so they would be happier in a home where there are people around for most of the day.

◄ This **eclectus parrot** is having fun playing with its toys.

Your bird's new home

Before you bring your pet home, make sure its cage is placed somewhere safe and away from draughts and hot spots such as radiators.

Large cage

It is always best to buy the largest cage possible for your pet. As a minimum, the bird must be able to stretch its wings. If the cage has wire bars, make sure they are close together so your pet cannot push its head through them and get stuck. Place the cage where your pet can see people, but keep it away from windows, draughty corners and banging doors.

Do it!

Checklist — things you will need for your new pet:
- Cage • Liner for cage
- Food container
- Water bottle
- Toys, such as a mirror and bell
- Cuttlefish bone
- Perches
- Bird sand

▲ Budgerigars should be let out of their cage to fly around at least once a day.

▲ Canaries in the wild (left) and the pet canary in its cage (right) use their sharp claws to grip on to a perch.

Bird safe

Before you bring your bird home, make sure the room where you plan to keep it is safe. Flying birds may crash into windows and mirrors, and get badly injured. Pull the curtains before you let your bird out, or put stickers on windows so your bird can see something is there, and cover mirrors.

Perches

In the wild, many birds perch on branches to rest. Their toes wrap around the branch and grip so they don't fall off when they sleep. Make sure your bird's cage has perches of different sizes as this helps them to exercise their feet.

Caring for your pet

Keeping birds is easy, as long as you follow a few basic rules to keep them happy, safe and healthy.

Fresh food and water

Give your pet fresh food and water every day. Most birds prefer to drink from a water bottle rather than a bowl. Wash the bottle and food container every week.

PET POINT
Your pet bird may be scared of other pets, especially cats and dogs. Make sure these pets are out of the room when you clean your bird's cage, or let it fly around out of its cage.

Snack time

Sprays of **millet** are great snacks for your pet. Millet seeds are low in fat and will help to keep your pet healthy. Other healthy snacks include fruit such as apples.

◄ Regularly replace food treats, such as millet sticks, which birds like to peck.

Weekly jobs

Each week, wipe the bars of the cage and clean out the tray at the bottom. Wash the perches and any toys, too. Every month you need to remove your bird and give the cage a thorough clean. Always wash your hands after cleaning your bird's tray or cage.

▲ Give your pet some water in a solid shallow bowl so it can enjoy a bath. Change this bath every week.

Tray liner

Place a liner in the tray at the bottom of your bird's cage to catch its droppings. This needs to be changed daily so your pet does not have to walk in its own droppings.

◀ Tray liners are made from sandpaper. They should be changed every day.

Handling your pet

You need to be able to handle your bird so you can easily move it in and out of its cage, or take it to the vet.

Picking up birds

Large birds are easier to pick up. Make sure you tuck in their wings and keep their head away from your face. Small birds are trickier to handle. You need to take some time to get your pet used to you before you handle it.

Do it!

Make sure all the windows and doors are closed before you take your bird out of its cage.

◀ Never hold a bird, such as this lovebird, around its chest as it will not be able to breathe.

Calming talk

Birds get stressed easily, and talking helps to calm them down. Talk to your bird so it gets used to your voice. Next, give your pet a treat so it gets used to your hand. Then you can start to handle your pet.

▶ Give your bird a treat, such as a piece of fruit, when you are training it.

Step up!

Handling your bird is much easier if you train it to step on to your hand. Slowly extend your hand into its cage. Don't rush or your bird will get scared. Press your finger on to its belly just above its legs and it should step on to your finger. At the same time say 'step up', and the bird will learn to do this.

◀ Your bird's feet and claws may feel a little scratchy at first, but you'll soon get used to them.

Health checks

A healthy bird has clean, shiny feathers, eats well and is very active. Check your bird every day to make sure it is looking well.

Is my bird sick?

It is easy to tell if your bird is not well. It will sit at the bottom of its cage with its feathers **ruffled**. It may sneeze or have runny eyes and nostrils. It may make a **rasping** sound as it breathes. There may be droppings stuck to its tail feathers. If you think your pet is ill, tell an adult and take it to the vet for a check-up.

PET POINT

Some books tell people to use sandpaper perches to keep the bird's nails short. But this is more likely to cause sores on your pet's feet.

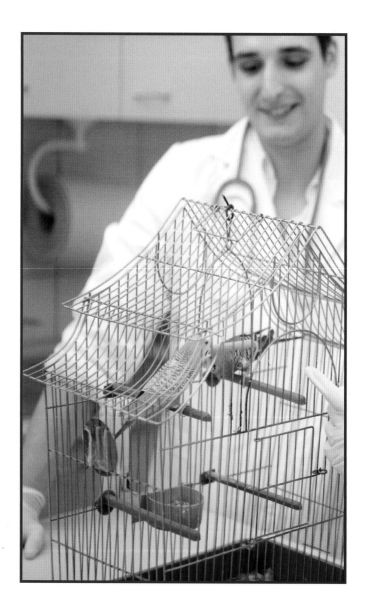

▲ Make sure your pet cannot escape on the way to see the vet. Take it in a cage or a small pet carrier.

Get a trim

Some birds need their nails trimmed regularly. For example, parrots grow long nails that can be painful when they sit on your arm or shoulder.

Birds use their beaks to **preen** their feathers, so if your bird's beak becomes overgrown or cracked, it needs to be trimmed. Take your bird to the vet for regular nail and beak trimming.

◀ A healthy bird, such as this Amazon parrot, has clean eyes, smooth feathers, a trimmed beak and nails, and looks alert.

▲ This rainbow lorikeet is using its beak to keep its feathers clean.

Life Cycle

Female birds lay eggs and some hatch into young birds called chicks. Parent birds care for their young until the chicks are ready to fly away.

▲ Parrots and parakeets, such as this red-fronted parakeet, build their nests in holes in trees.

Nest building

Most wild birds build a nest in which to lay their eggs. Nests are made from materials, such as twigs and leaves, moss or mud, and are lined with **downy** feathers. Pet birds make their nests in a nest box or on the floor of their cage.

Incubation

Female birds lay their eggs and then sit on them to keep them warm. This is called **incubation**. The chicks hatch a few weeks later. Many people collect the eggs from their pet birds and put them in an **incubator**. After they hatch, the chicks are fed by hand rather than by the parent birds.

Cockatiel life cycle

A female **cockatiel** is ready to breed at about a year old. She lays up to 8 eggs, which hatch after 21 days. The chicks have a yellow-pink skin with a few feathers. Both parents feed the chicks by coughing up food from their own stomach. The chicks' eyes open after about 10 days. Their feathers grow quickly and they are able to fly by 5 weeks of age. Their parents feed them until they learn to do it themselves. The young birds leave their parents at about 3 months of age. Cockatiels can live for about 20 years.

10-day-old chick

8-week-old chicks

young adult

Caring for chicks

Birds are good parents and look after their chicks, protecting them and bringing them food. Some chicks are born naked and blind. Their parents keep them warm and feed them. Within a few weeks, the chicks have grown their feathers and are ready to leave the nest.

▶ Blackbirds catch worms, caterpillars and small insects to feed their chicks.

Beaks and food

A bird's beak is shaped to help it eat the type of food it likes, so you can tell what sort of food a bird eats by looking at its beak.

Seed eaters

A seed-eating bird has a short, sturdy beak to crush tough seeds. Birds that are **predators**, such as owls and eagles, have a large, hooked beak to catch and hold prey. **Humming birds** and sunbirds have a long beak to push into flowers. Then they use their long tongue to lap up the sugary **nectar**.

▲ The hyacinth macaw (above) uses its strong beak to crush palm fruits. These pet **conures** (left) have a similar-shaped beak, which helps them to break open tough seeds and nuts.

Fruit and veg

Many people think pet birds eat only seeds, but most eat a mix of fruit, leafy vegetables, seeds and even cheese and hard-boiled egg. Wild birds love to eat fruit, just like their pet cousins.

PET POINT

Never feed your pet bird chocolate, avocado, apple seeds (the fruit is okay), tomatoes or salt, as these foods are bad for them.

◀ This budgerigar is eating a variety of small seeds, which it crushes and opens with its beak.

Ready-made foods

There are lots of different packaged foods for pet birds, each prepared to suit a particular type or species. Often, food mixes contain added minerals and vitamins to make sure your bird stays healthy. Seed-eaters, such as budgerigars, canaries and finches, need a mix of seeds each day, including millet and sunflower. It is best to buy a ready-made mix of seeds for your pet.

21

Wild cousins

 Pet birds may live in cages or aviaries, but they still have much in common with their wild cousins.

Living in a flock

Many wild birds live in groups called flocks. A flock of birds stays together all the time. They fly and feed together, and protect each other from predators. Most pet birds like company and need to be with other birds. They also enjoy being handled, and they like to play and be stroked.

▼ In Australia, it is common to see flocks of wild rainbow lorikeets in towns and gardens.

The wild monk parakeet (left) is enjoying a tasty meal of fruits. The pet African grey parrot (right) has found a peanut to eat.

▼ Many owners cover their pet's cage at night to keep out the light so the bird can sleep.

Keeping busy

In the wild, birds spend a lot of time searching for food. Your pet will enjoy having toys to play with and food to 'find', so hang some pieces of food in its cage. Make sure old food is cleared away at the end of each day.

Sleeping in the wild

Most birds are active during the day and sleep at night, except for a few **nocturnal** species, such as owls, that hunt at night. When it gets dark, birds roost (rest) in trees or creep into hollows in tree trunks. Pet birds need to sleep at night, too. Some roost on their perches or sit on the cage floor.

Bird talk

Birds communicate with each other in many ways, but the most common is by using sound. Some have a sweet song; others a loud squawk!

Bird song

Songbirds, such as blackbirds and skylarks, make the most amazing sounds. Male birds sing to tell other males that they are there, and to attract females.

▼ Cockerels (left) make a loud crowing noise, especially at dawn when they wake up. Robins (right) communicate with twitters, tweets and song.

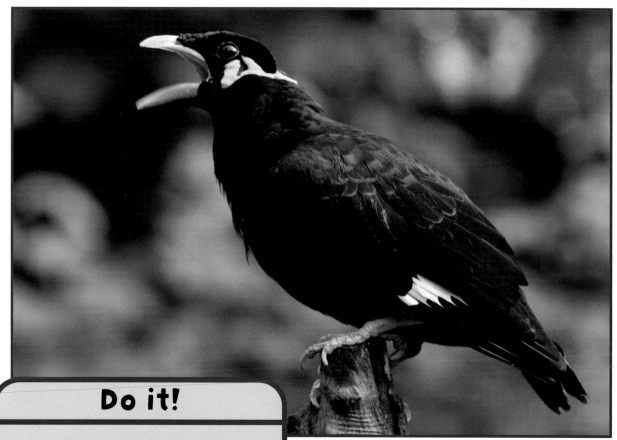

Do it!

Some birds repeat words that they hear. If you want your pet to say something, repeat the word clearly many times to encourage it to say it back.

▲ **Mynah birds mimic** human voices, and some pet birds can be taught words, sentences and even songs.

Bird calls

Birds that do not sing make calls instead. There are many types of call, each with a different meaning. Alarm calls alert other birds of danger. Birds call to each other when flying in a flock, and young chicks make peeps when they are calling out for their parents.

Talking birds

Starlings are brilliant mimics, copying the song of other birds and other sounds, such as sheep and buses. Pet birds do this too, mimicking the sounds that their owners make. The best pet mimic is the mynah bird. Other pets that are good at talking are parrots, macaws and budgerigars.

Instant expert

There are about 10,000 species of bird in the world. Wild birds can be found in all **habitats**, from jungles and deserts to the frozen **Arctic**.

The biggest ....

The biggest bird is the **ostrich**. It is so tall and heavy that it cannot fly. It grows to more than 2.7 metres in height and weighs a massive 150 kg or more. Even its eggs are huge, each weighing about 1.4 kg – that's the same as about 28 hen's eggs.

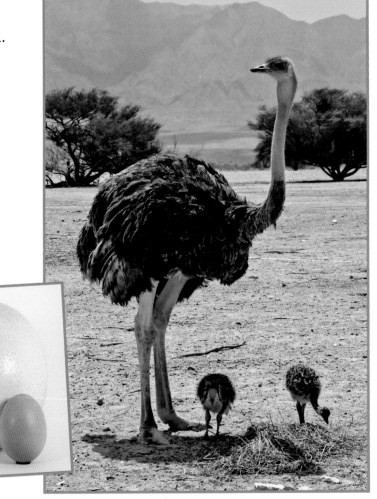

▶ A hen's egg looks tiny next to the huge ostrich egg. The tiny ostrich chicks (far right) will soon grow into strong birds.

...and the smallest

The male bee hummingbird is tiny, just 5 cm long and weighing only 1.8 grams. It comes from Cuba in the Caribbean.

The fastest

The fastest bird is the **peregrine falcon**, which dives down to catch its prey, reaching speeds of 320 km per hour.

Extreme fliers

The **Arctic tern** flies from the Arctic to the **Antarctic** and back every year – a distance of more than 38,000 km. Some terns are known to have flown about 80,000 km in a year.

▲ Arctic terns fly huge distances every year.

▲ Lovebirds are popular pets. They get their name from the way they behave. When they are kept in pairs, they sit close together and constantly groom each other.

▲ The **wandering albatross** spends most of its life flying over the ocean.

FAST FACT

A small song bird, such as a robin, has about 4,000 feathers. A swan that lives in the Arctic has 25,000 feathers to help keep it warm.

Largest wingspan

The wandering albatross has the longest wingspan, up to 3.7 metres from tip to tip. Albatrosses are expert gliders, staying in the air for hours without beating their wings. They even sleep while they fly.

pet quiz

Now you know a bit more about what is involved in looking after birds, is a bird the right pet for you?

1. How often should your bird be allowed out of its cage?
- **a)** It doesn't need to be let out, because it's got a big cage
- **b)** About once a week
- **c)** At least once a day

2. How long can a budgerigar live?
- **a)** Not very long
- **b)** About 5 years
- **c)** About 25 years

3. How big should your bird's cage be?
- **a)** Not very big
- **b)** Just larger than the bird
- **c)** Big enough so it can spread its wings

4. If you see your pet bird sitting on the floor of its cage with its feathers ruffled, is it
- **a)** Sleeping
- **b)** Resting
- **c)** Unwell

5. How much time do you have to spend with your pet each day?
- **a)** Not much, I'm very busy
- **b)** I can spend lots of time with it at weekends
- **c)** I'll spend some time with it every day

See page 32 to find out if a bird is the right pet for you.

Owning a pet — checklist

All pets need to be treated with respect. Remember your pet bird can feel pain and distress.

To be a good pet owner you should remember these five rules. Make sure your pet:

- never suffers from fear and distress
- is never hungry or thirsty
- never suffers discomfort
- is free from pain, injury and disease
- and has freedom to show its normal behaviour

To keep your pet healthy and happy you have to check it at least twice a day to make sure it has enough fresh water and food.

You must keep your bird's cage or aviary clean. Check its cage or aviary to make sure there is nothing there that may hurt it and that it cannot escape. Also, make sure no other pets or animals can harm or scare your bird.

Make sure your pet's cage is not in direct sunlight or above a hot radiator. Do not keep the cage next to a noisy radio or television.

You must remember to buy new supplies of its food in time so that your pet never goes hungry.

Your bird must have enough space to fly, and it should be allowed to fly out of its cage at least once a day for about an hour. Make sure that rooms are made bird-safe before letting your pet fly indoors.

If your pet bird becomes ill or hurts itself tell an adult and take your pet to be checked by a vet.

Glossary

Antarctic the region around the South Pole

Arctic the region around the North Pole

Arctic tern a type of seabird that breeds in the Arctic

aviary a huge space with shelter, usually outdoors, where many birds are kept and where they can fly around

bred the careful selection of parents to produce young with special features

breeder a person who keeps animals, such as pet birds, to breed and sell

captivity when wild animals are kept in places such as parks or zoos, and are not free to roam in their natural habitat

cockatiels small grey Australian parrots with a yellow crest of feathers on the head

cockatoos a type of parrot, usually with white feathers and a colourful crest of feathers on the head

conures small to medium-sized parakeets from Central and South America

domesticated tamed and used to living with people

downy soft and fluffy

eclectus parrot a small parrot from Northern Australia, New Guinea and islands of the Pacific Ocean

exotic strange, unusual, from a different part of the world

habitats the places or surroundings in which animals live

hummingbirds tiny birds that can hover in front of flowers. They get their name from the 'hum' that their wings make when they beat them quickly

incubation keeping an egg or young warm so it will develop and grow

incubator a device that is used to hatch eggs by keeping them warm.

macaws large, brightly coloured parrots with long tail feathers, from Central and South America

millet a type of grain, like wheat and oats

mimic to copy and imitate

mynah birds Asian birds related to the starling that are good mimics

nectar a sugary liquid produced by some flowers

nocturnal active at night

ostrich the largest living bird; a flightless bird with long legs

parakeets small parrots with long tail feathers, such as budgerigars

perch (verb) to rest on a branch; (noun) a branch that a bird uses to rest on

peregrine falcon a bird of prey, with long, pointed wings, capable of fast flight

predator an animal that hunts and eats other animals

preen to clean and smooth feathers with a beak

rasping a scraping sound

ruffled when feathers are out of place or roughed up

tamed no longer wild

tropical part of the world near the Equator where the climate is hot and wet

wandering albatross a large seabird that spends most of its life at sea. It flies around the southern oceans

wingspan the distance from one wingtip to the other

zebra finches small seed-eating birds. They are found in Central Australia and Indonesia

Index

Pet quiz – results

If you answered **(c)** to most of the questions then a bird could be for you.